METANOIA
μετάνοια

pronounced "metAnia"

A change of thinking.
An *entirely* new way of life.
A transformation in thinking.

"What does it matter if the whole world cries out against you if you are right"

Marcus Aurelius

METANOIA

THE ART OF TRANSMUTATION

Jay Carson

A HANDBOOK

Quantum Mind – Quantum Healing®

First Edition

The information in this book is for information and discussion purposes only. It does not propose that the reader adopt the ideas or undertake the exercises described in this book and it does not replace medical or mental health advice. The information in this book is not for the diagnosis, prescription or treatment of any health disorder whatsoever. It is not meant to replace or supersede any individual person's medical or professional health practitioner. The author and publisher are in no way liable for any misuse of the material in this book. Please seek professional advice in all situations.

Bibliographies:

The works of Nancy Appleton, John Bennet, Alice Bailey, Edgar Cayce, Rodney Collins, Samuel Copely, George Gurdjieff, Julian Johnson, Evarts Loomis, Maurice Nicoll, Peter Ouspensky, Sig Paulson, Beryl Pogson, Walter Reed, Walter Russel, Jeanne de Salzman, Idries Shah, Russel Targ, and the Upanishads.

If a quote appears, in this book, from an author I have not included in the above biography please accept my apologies and any reader or publisher may contact me immediately so that I can include the author's name. This is a work in progress and is part of a larger document which undergoes continuous development.

Copyright © 2009, 2011 by Jay Carson

All rights reserved
Copyright throughout the world

No part of this publication may be reproduced or transmitted in any form or by any means, electronic, mechanical or photographic, by recording or any information storage or retrieval system or method now known or to be invented or adapted, without the prior permission obtained in writing from the author.

First published in 2009 in note form.

First Edition published in 2011

Quantum Mind – Quantum Healing Series

ISBN 978-0-9870098-0-7

Quantum Mind – Quantum Healing®

I have been criticized for being a wayfarer, as though this made me the less worthy. Let no one hold it against me if I defend myself against such allegations.

The journeys I have made up until now have been very useful to me, because no man's master grows in his own house, nor has anyone found his teacher behind his stove.

Paracelsus

*When the camel of our efforts sinks into the mud,
what matter whether the destination is near or far?*

Ustad Khalilullah Khalili

for Marilyn

Metanoia - The Art of Transmutation

To find yourself

Think for yourself

Socrates

***In order to think for yourself
you "need to clear your mind of rubbish"
and 'reverse your usual way of looking at things.'***

CONTENTS

Preface	10
Introduction	13
Intuition (see Definitions)	19
Definitions	19
Consciousness	22
Understanding	25
Intuition, Events, Impressions and Suggestions	27
The Mistakes of Others	34
Identification and Fascination	35
Mental Prisons and Centres of Gravity	36
The (so called) Subconscious Mind	37
Provocation and Bitterness	38
Negativity	41
Culture and the Basics	43
What's in a Word?	49
Time	53
Suffering and Emotions	54
Speed and Haste	58
Who are You?	59
Judgement and Criticism	62
Who are We?	63
Duality, Non-Duality and Polarization	65
Aspects of Healing	68
The Way to Liberation	70
Introduction II	77
Energy Transfer	81
The Relationship between Life and Non-locality	82
The Quiet Mind	86
Perspectives on Life	87
Attitude as a Creative Tool	88
Illness or Dis-ease	93
Forgiveness and Fear	96

PREFACE

A warning - This little book is not for everyone.

This book is about continuous dedication and discipline. It is about using each event in our lives (whether it be big or small, positive or negative in nature) to learn "control over ourselves", learning to distinguish the "real from the illusory", and developing the ability to *feel* the truth.

In the words attributed to Socrates (but most likely from a much earlier period) and Hakim Sanai this book is about:

"Self- knowledge and giving attention to the soul"
and the realization that,

"Knowledge that does not take you beyond yourself is worse than ignorance."

To gain knowledge of yourself requires amongst many other things, knowledge of **the way of thinking** of the culture and society from which you come, and the organisational culture and environment in which you were educated.

To know and understand yourself includes knowing how you think, what and why you think about others, and seeing and hearing yourself through the eyes and ears of others.

However, "self-deception often prevents knowledge".

Therefore before you gain knowledge of who you are (that is, the real *you*, which we shall term your 'essence' or true Self) you need to gain knowledge of and understand the current you, and the possibly many other 'you's' or 'faces', or I's that you present to the world and use to interact with the world before you.

Similar to the well trained horses of a charioteer these other 'you's or I's must be trained to obey the real you (ie Self) when you adjust the reins. Otherwise they will pull the Self in whatever direction takes their fancy.

The aim is to expose you to possible different ways to bring about radical change in your understanding and perception of yourself. It is a preparation for learning. One of the ways to achieve this aim is to help you learn to bring about changes in your reactions to situations and how you view yourself in relation to the world at large.

Remember, these changes will not take place overnight and the way is long. There are no short cuts. It is a matter of daily practice. And even when you think or feel you have achieved a higher level of consciousness you will suddenly find that you have to start from scratch again. In the words of Collins based on the work of Ouspensky "They realized that in the way of development true knowledge must first be acquired and then abandoned. That exactly what makes possible the opening of one door may make impossible the opening of the next."

Terms such as finding oneself, living in the present, mindfulness, consciousness or whatever similar term is currently fashionable have spawned numerous films, books, videos, seminars and talks. However, after the initial euphoria or excitement of a particular film or book many people discover that it is very difficult to start to even attempt to achieve the life depicted, let alone actually achieve that new life.

Often it may be due to the fact that before a person can begin to learn 'new' (in fact very old) things he or she usually has to get rid of many old ideas, concepts and stored (mental) programs. That is, we need to get rid of old mental clutter

Therefore, the aim is to identify approaches that will help you begin to remove the clutter that may hinder new learning. Consider a mental and emotional awakening as possible in any environment in which you may live, and whatever your background. However, it is not an easy task no matter what the popular novels and videos may depict.

There are times when certain statements or paragraphs in this book may appear contradictory. Why? - Because the context may have changed. In addition, at times, you need to give up or abandon what you have learnt in order to learn new things. Often, in order to make progress, you have to abandon certain past habits, thoughts and learning.

Metanoia and The Art of Transmutation (1st Edition), Quantum Mind – Quantum Healing series is of an *introductory and fundamental nature.*

Consider the development of the thoughts expressed in this book as precursor or prerequisite for those actively seeking self-development and personal growth.

"Have you leather?"

"Yes"

"And nails?"

"Yes"

"And dye?"

"Yes"

"Then why don't you make yourself a pair of boots"

Mulla Nasrudin

INTRODUCTION

Self-realization can be very demanding and usually requires radical changes to a person's way of life.

One method to help you along the road to self-awareness or self-realization is self-observation (SO) which is the registering (without self-analysis or criticism) of how you operate and interact with the world.

A person who is experienced in self-observation (SO) has no need for 'learning-aids' because the process is totally integrated into his or her life. That is, it becomes a "complete experience" because the process of observing or seeing is not the observing. It is an act or experience that only takes place when there is 'no separation between what sees and what is seen." That is, there exists "no point from which the observation is made."

There are times when statements or comments in this book, may appear contradictory which is another reason to re-read and re-read. In addition many of the "exercises" may appear, to someone experienced in such matters, to be incorrect or modified (in the strict sense), or a reader may say "that is not the way it should be done" or "I would not do it that way".

Therefore my request is, "Have a little patience." If, for example, a person struggles with the idea of self-observation I suggest the creation and use of an external mental or virtual observer when a person starts to practice self-observation.

The 'aid' (of a person observing him or her self via the use of an external mental observer) is just that – a temporary aid to get the student started along the way.

There is a trend to equate the endless reading of the latest books, watching the latest DVDs and films, attending the latest 'in vogue' seminar on metaphysics or new age thinking with experience. That is, reading, watching and listening have become a substitute for practical experience.

There is no substitute for extensive, wide-ranging and intense practical experience with respect to both the student and the teacher.

There is a further trend supported by TV and the internet for skilfully presented *opinion* to become 'facts' in the minds of many viewers and readers.

Many people then act and make decisions on the basis of these 'facts' not understanding that they are acting on an opinion and only an opinion no matter how skilfully and persuasively presented. There are times when subsequent actions or statements, based on opinion not facts, may be detrimental in both the short and long term.

This book is of a practical nature in that the emphasis is about the *application* of the ideas or philosophies rather than the principles behind the ideas described in this book.

It is about the application of certain basic principles without, initially, seeking to discover the deeper meanings. The rationale behind this approach is twofold:

1) The application alone will slowly lift the many veils which currently restrict the vision of many people to what is directly before them but cannot be seen.

2) The lifting of the veils gives the student both the motivation and the hints as to where to first seek the doors and then the keys to each door, each in turn, to a place where both the 'future' and 'time' unfold in a way unimaginable before.

At first reading this book may appear very basic and simplistic, however the key, as in many other walks of life, is in the continuous application of what is read, not the words themselves. The approach is that understanding and appreciation develop over time, as a direct result *of* the application of ideas, beliefs or philosophies.

Without application and understanding they (words) are simply, "words, words, words."

The emphasis is on simple tools that will help deconstruct or understand past conditioning and inappropriate logic that may often control and influence various aspects of many people's lives.

The methods suggested and described are simple and basic but the application thereof takes great patience and practice (devotion).The philosophy of transformation as described in this book is one of constant practice and self-observation (without analysis or criticism) and has no place for assumptions, speculation or rumour or opinion based on hearsay, or on what you read in newspapers or internet, or hear on the TV.

Therefore, in the context of this book the Greek 'Logos' is translated to mean, "The essence of all meaning."

If your interest is in, for example, new-age astral travel (after reading a single book or watching a DVD), enjoying the latest version of westernised yoga or hot yoga, or the development of an external image of serenity or peace this book is *not* for you. Neither is it for the "immature, lazy or superstitious."

If you wish to learn to take full responsibility for your own actions the ideas in this book will help you. One of the aims is to emphasize the need to stop old, conditioned, reflex actions to external events over which we have no control. It is the nature of the reaction to the event rather than the event itself that turns into a 'problem'.

The methods, ideas, concepts, and exercises you will read about may be used during specific discussions and group meetings, which are meant to, "Create conditions in which a man has a better chance of awakening himself. A teacher cannot awaken anybody." Only you can find the answers.

The workshops associated with this book are by nature very low key yet dynamic and interactive, and the notes in this book are often only briefly referred to. Therefore, this book can be of benefit when read 'alone' without attending a workshop. It must be stressed that the ideas that may be gained from this book require more than one reading (of this book). You may want to take this book to work or read while travelling on a bus or train.

Certain questions may be posed in various sections of the text the answers of which, from the perspective of the author, are available via email. You are encouraged to provide your own answers before requesting 'answers' via email.

There are sections of text that may at times appear vague or incomplete. The reason is that you are encouraged to provide your own thoughts and ideas at that particular point in the reading.

If you wish to discuss any aspect of this book you may do so via Skype or email. A Skype address will be provided via email.

It is important to remember that this is *not* a 'cookbook' that lays out each step and process in a sequential manner. It is not an academic or scholarly work. It is simply a collection of ideas or philosophies for discussion.

There is no order to this book. At times statements in different sections may contradict themselves – it depends on the context.

This book offers no quick fixes, no *instant* improvements in life and it contains no secrets. Carry it in your bag or pocket. Do not waste your time trying to analyse the contents of this book. Simply treat it as a 'taster', similar to tasting wine. It is a simple little mirror that will help you possibly see yourself every day in a new light.

If you are asked a question (in the book) answer the question not once but many times over a period of weeks, months, even years. You may be surprised at the answers, and how your answers may change.

Remember, it is written in a casual, conversational style. It is not academic in any way. Warning: The words 'you', 'they', 'others' often appear in the text. Read slowly and carefully as these words do serve a purpose although not obvious at first reading.

For a workshop in your country or town send an email to: magicorum@gmail.com

*"Very little is needed to make a happy life;
it is all within yourself, in your way of thinking"*

Marcus Aurelius

"A Disciple –
Sir, Teach me more of the knowledge of Brahman.

The Master –
I have told you the secret knowledge. Austerity, self-control, performance of duty without attachment – these are the body of that knowledge."

The Upanishads

DEFINITIONS
(in the context of this book)

Intuition

The term or word *intuition* is much misused - we could say even abused in the last few years. In the context of this book and depending on the context in which it is used consider **intuition** as:

a) The ability to recognise your *own* essence.

b) Understanding the essence of life - human or otherwise.

c) A higher force sometimes called a fourth force (Jung) which appears when man has internal harmony (equal control and balance of all his thoughts, emotions, feelings, desires, cravings, wants and actions).

d) "..that state .. in which our thought is no longer divided into a thinking subject and an external world, but rather the outer world is abolished by its integration in our personal consciousness."

e) **Not** present when rationality and logic dominate.

f) (Street Wisdom) - When you know whether a statement is fact, fiction or opinion *before* a person opens his or her mouth to make the statement. Consider,

> *"He who depends upon his eyes for sight, his ears for hearing and his mouth for speech, he is still dead."*
> (Hazrat Inayat Khan)

Intuition cannot be taught. No one can teach you intuition. Only you can awaken or develop your intuition. One of the aims of this booklet is to help you to start to learn how you can start to awaken your intuition. Remember, there are no shortcuts – re-read c) above.

Essence: That which is your own (comes from inside and is not created by external impressions of the world or learnt from outside sources)

Personality: That which is based on learning that comes from the outside (parents, school, university, business organizations, sports groups etc.). That which is developed based on the influence and opinion of other people, development based on imitation of other people.

[This may not be a definition of 'personality' you would normally expect]

Text-Box, Highlighted Text or *Italics*: When you see text within a box, highlighted text or text in *italics* please consider or interpret the text as depicting choices or alternatives that appear before you every day. [SO, correctly practiced and over time, will slowly improve the 'quality' of the choices that you make. It will also make different or new alternatives appear which you did not notice before].

?: When you see a '?' (which is not at the end of a question) it implies that you should add your own comments or thoughts. (If you should wish to discuss your comments or thoughts simply email to arrange a time to Skype)

Association/associate/identification/identify: These words apply (in the context of this book) when negative thoughts arise when you see people or hear people that you do not know or know nothing about. A simple example: you may see people (whom you have never seen before) in a restaurant and hear them talking. For some reason the way they are dressed, their mannerisms, the manner in which they talk, or what they say may annoy or irritate you in some way although you know absolutely nothing about them - this is a simple example of association or 'to associate' or 'identify' or identification with a person or a group of people.

Self-Observation, Self-Observe, Self-Observing (SO): An all-day every day, impartial, uncritical, non-analytical study of your behaviour, thoughts, emotions, actions and reactions. It includes becoming aware of all your internal impulses and their outward manifestations and most importantly ***without criticism or analysis***. Self-Observation truly practiced continuously over long periods automatically (in the background, subconsciously) modifies negative behaviour or thoughts.

As a famous golfer once said, "The more I practice the luckier I get", or words to that effect.

The approach suggested (in this book) is one approach to starting SO. Also, it is only an introduction. Please reread the comments about SO in the introduction.

Self-Remembering (SR): Is the process of dividing your attention into internal and external perspectives of yourself in order to connect with the energy of consciousness. When people have achieved self-remembering it can be said that they have reached a certain level of consciousness and are, for example, able to see deep into themselves, understand the rationale for their behaviour and values, and are conscious of the harm they may have caused to themselves or others in the past.

Note:

In the context of this booklet we will primarily use the term Self-Observation (SO). However, consider SO integral to Self-Remembering (SR) and, at times and again in the context of this work-book, interchangeable with SR.

Consider the practice of Self-Observation as the means to achieve Self-Remembering.

Therefore a suggestion, read this book at least twice, hopefully a thousand times.

Conditioning: How you are influenced in thought and behaviour by your: peers, parents, school, university, friends, relations, culture, organisations (work, profession, social), TV, internet, print media, etc.

Consciousness:

How do you, "express that which is almost inexpressible"?

Remember to read between the lines.

Remember what is *not* said may be more important than what is said.

Remember the spaces between objects may be more important than the 'objects'. Keep looking or keep listening.

Negative Emotions (-E):

Examples of negative emotions are: Irritability, impatience, anger, fear, self-pity, jealousy, greed, hatred, intolerance, etc.

Consciousness

CONSCIOUSNESS – (in western literature another much abused word or term) a few 'definitions' '

A traditional medical or linear definition –

> *'Consciousness is the critical biological function that allows us to know sorrow, or know joy, to know suffering or know pleasure.'*
> Prof Antonio Damasio

A non-linear, non-local view –

> *'Consciousness and non-locality are when a person's thoughts and intentions are instinctively linked to nature and the universe.'*
> Dr R. Targ

'Consciousness is a state in which a man knows all at once everything that in general he knows and in which he can see how little he does know and how many contradictions there are in what he knows.'
G.I. Gurdjieff

'When a person's thoughts and intentions are **not** *instinctively linked to nature and the universe' he is 'nothing but infinitely small particles on the surface of a grain of dust lost in the immensity of the cosmos.'*
Street Philosophy by Dr Jay Carson
[compiled from the views of to Dr R.Targ and Dr A.Carrel (Nobel Laureate 1873-1944)]

In cosmic terms –

Consciousness: Indefinable and non-measurable.

'I regard consciousness as fundamental. I regard matter as derivative from consciousness.'
Max Plank

Brahman – The inexpressible the indescribable – the ultimate.
Hinduism

"*Consciousness – "Knowing together" - all the centres working in harmony, working as pilot and inspiration. Being "very sensitive to the appropriateness of time and place for different manifestations"*
Dr M. Nicoll

"*Consciousness might be defined as the faculty of apprehension, and concerns primarily the relation of the Self to the not-self, of the Knower to the Known, and the Thinker to that which is thought.*"
Alice Bailey

"We know what we are, but not what we may be.'

Hamlet

A modern version of Hamlet's quote should read

*"We **think** we know what or who we are, and we do not work enough at what we may be."*

Understanding

'Understanding' grows only with the growth of 'being'. Growth of 'being' comes from self-observation and self-remembering. Therefore, any 'feelings of loneliness or detachment' are always opportunities for 'self- observation'. The way to liberation is, "Know thyself"

Information (data) is *not* Knowledge. Knowledge requires Understanding. Understanding requires Knowledge.

Remember, no one else can experience what you feel or experience. A person may 'think' and may even say that he or she can feel or experience what another person 'feels' - this is not possible except by a very few rare individuals. Happiness, sadness, anxiety, depression are very personal things.

In the past you may have been asked:

What would you really, truly like to do, perform, work? What is your hidden talent? Do you have a talent, latent, hidden or even obvious and known to you and others but not utilised?

These are traditional linear questions the aim of which may be to help you set goals or purpose in life. However, it is also possible they may take you *nowhere* because you may still be influenced by past conditioning.

Continuously look for situations, processes, movements, words with which you are *not* normally involved in order to gain 'new impressions' of yourself and clear your head of old nonsense.

Intuition, Events, Impressions and Suggestions

Events of some sort or another occur every day at home and at work.

Discussion:

The destruction of intuition.

The greater the decline of intuition the greater the decline of man.

Once intuition is lost, ALL is lost. Why? because intuition is "doing the right thing".

Many factors, variables (particularly 'western', logic based education) contribute to the loss of intuition.

Intuition is an integral aspect of man's essence. However, his personality (a result of conditioning – education, peers, culture, parents, training …) often dampens intuition.

Once your intuition is totally dampened you become a robot dependent upon pure logic and past conditioning (education, training, etc.)

Therefore, consider: Is your education, training appropriate to *yourself* or a given event.

> *"Do **not** react to antagonism or provocation"*
>
> and
>
> *"Accept what each and every moment has to offer and utilise that moment to its fullest degree in order to develop and evolve"*

In some situations our personality (our training, our conditioning, our culture) may over-react in an inappropriate manner [positively or negatively] when faced with a difficult situation or person.

If faced with a sudden, difficult or awkward situation [that is not life threatening and does not require immediate action] - force yourself to laugh mentally or physically and say to yourself I am going to learn from this situation and Self-Observe.

SO every minute of every day

Responsibility

New perspectives sometimes help free us from the past. For example, for some people, it will help stop them repeating the same mistakes over and over. Instead, they start to make wise choices.

"The ultimate responsibility for any negative emotion – anger, irritation, fear, self-pity and so on rests with the individual rather than the events that befall him." We also have a responsibility to ourselves to stop what appears to be our endless pursuit of more speed, and to **stop all referrals or stories about past wrongs or problems experienced.**

> *Stop all judgment and criticism*
> *Only use positive responses*

I am sure we all know a person who has spent months, years sometimes even a lifetime blaming others or some past event for a current situation. However, over time, we can transform or stop any existing or habitual reactions to past or perceived suffering by self-observation (SO).

SO and SR are ancient techniques to help a person enjoy the present and receive all the benefits of the present. SO and SR are central to the development of consciousness and awareness.

For many individuals the mind and the body have been conditioned (via many factors) to march to the beat of many drums – usually not their own. Speed and more speed are the order of the day. Simple example – many people have developed the habit of speaking very quickly and in their 'minds' they 'understand' what they mean or are trying to express. However, in their haste to express themselves they may construct sentences that distort what they are trying to impart and in doing so do not convey any real message to the listener.

One way to stop hurrying is to accept that in the bigger picture to each and every one of us - the *"next moment is no greater than the present moment"*. We are not talking about life or death situations where every second counts. We are talking about an awareness of life – we may 'hurry' at times when it is necessary but we must not let it take control of our lives. If we are not in control the result may be constant mental agitation, and a mind that is always a little irritated by small delays or deviations to what is expected or wanted, which in turn can impact on our immune system.

The continuous practice of SO helps us utilise and take advantage of suffering rather than being used by suffering. We have a responsibility to ourselves to SO. Being 'present' is one aspect of SO and is a tool to help achieve a higher level of consciousness. It means being fully conscious or sensitive to your environment and the people around you during your daily life. This is not an easy task and for some may take years of practice. Reading a book, watching a film, attending a seminar or retreat will not make it happen overnight. It takes practice and more practice.

Any and every emotional upheaval or negative thought is an opportunity to Self-Observe. When you have negative thoughts you are not in control and you are simply acting, talking, thinking according to a programme that is based on past events (old instructions that are out of date). Suddenly, similar to a computer, some hidden virus has started a hidden program and *it* is now in control.

Looking…

[Just looking at a beautiful view or looking at an arrangement of flowers or at a painting helps]

Every morning use this phrase,

> *'The events and experiences of today constitute my life'.*

We all work towards achieving what is loosely defined as consciousness, self-realization, enlightenment or awareness as if it was some *future event*.

> **"we cannot experience the future without penetrating and experiencing the present, for the present is the future."**

This does not mean that you sit and contemplate the 'present'; it simply means that you consider everything around *you as you go* through your normal day.

Obviously, some may consider sitting by the sea or on the top of a mountain as an ideal way or approach. However, this approach is not always convenient or practical.

Method…

Your continuous aim should be to "look and listen with active eyes and ears". This means that when you are in conversation with another person you should look and listen and not be thinking about what to say before the other person has stopped talking. Your eyes and ears must work intelligently not passively. Even your taste buds must work when you eat. Remember to taste and experience your food.

When you talk to someone focus 101% on that person – with your eyes, ears *and* mind but not 'in the person's face'. Active but low key and unobtrusive. A direct gaze does **not** necessarily signify so called 'strength of character'. Remember, some individuals develop the art of the direct gaze to influence and manipulate people with whom they come into contact. For the receiver of the gaze it can result in 'fascination' - fascination with the 'amazing gaze". They are in a sense hooked and may be easily influenced by 'words' emitting from the gaze. We will discuss fascination later. (E.g. Films, books – getting lost in the character)

As you listen, in parallel, develop different perspectives of what the person may be saying, implying or suggesting but do ***not make any assumptions***.

Listen beyond the words. Consider inclination, expression and movement.

If you are the talker – Talk is cheap. Repeatedly talking about what we do or did is a great inhibitor unless there is a very specific reason, or to clarify a situation.

Metanoia - The Art of Transmutation

[Imagination is another great inhibitor]

"One must become the words rather than talk the words."

For example, if you do not agree with what someone says - keep quiet and move on to another subject or issue.

Or, if you feel you must disagree with what was said answer from a different perspective (but keep it short). Wait for a reaction.

Another example: When a person is confrontational or unexpectedly 'in your face', do not answer back in any way. *Ask a question* (relative to the issue at hand) that requires the person to clarify what the problem is all about. Keep asking questions.

Transform -E (<u>do not talk</u> about transforming -E)

How? Actively SO and indirectly transform negative emotions

Watch for signs of impatience at all times.

SO is a KISS experience. The minute you start to make it complicated your personality (past conditioning: school, parents, peers, university, work organizations, culture, etc.) has taken control and subconscious analysis, evaluation and criticism occurs.

Hydrogen and oxygen are two basic elements of physical life. Consider SO and SR as two basic elements that support the development of Self.

Remember each second of each day – Remember those who do not have food, shelter, transport, or help when they are ill.

Remember each second that you interact with someone.

Remember each sensation, taste, texture of what you eat or feel.

<u>**Consider Self-Observation as the process of being simultaneously and intensely aware of yourself, what you are viewing and with whom or what you are interacting.**</u>

Consider SO (your other self, observer) as a CCTV Camera – no analysis, no comment, no opinion

Let us say that if you interact with a person or persons or you watch or look at something *without being aware of yourself* THEN we could say that you are in a state of fascination. That is, you are mentally, emotionally and spiritually asleep or in a conditioned state. That is, in a state created by other individuals not of your own making.

SO is something that is done naturally without any change in your mannerism or the way in which you talk. It is not something you discuss over coffee or a meal. It is simply something that you practice without talking about it. It is a very private thing.

Do not express negativity or negative emotions.

Use each and every form of negativity, especially the negative words or actions of others, to eliminate your own negative thoughts. Consider SO as a constant process that takes place irrespective of place, time and circumstances.

Look at anything – flowers, the sea, clouds and simultaneously be aware that you ARE looking.

When you stop expressing –E it allows you to develop different perspectives of yourself and it increases your motivation and ability to SO

Meaningless conversations, vivid imagination, lying, negative thoughts and behaviour seem to fill many people's lives.

Some people may talk too much; some people may talk too little. SO when you listen, talk or interact with all types of people.

Some people may express negative emotions continuously, may talk endlessly, may let their imagination take control of their thoughts and words, and may often fabricate or lie about events – all negative activities that can be physically and emotionally draining.

Consider 'lying' as a form of *vanity*. It is making statements or expressing opinions about things, people or places of which the speaker has no real knowledge, understanding or experience. Often people make statements in a manner that gives the impression that they 'know' about the things they have said when in reality they do not. It may be based on a story repeated by various 'theys' or something the person has read in a newspaper or magazine.

For a few minutes:

Let us consider what you 'know' as Knowledge (K) – you may know a lot of things (facts, figures, the rules of a particular sport, etc).

Let us consider what you 'understand' as Understanding (U) – the things that you really understand (ie have a comprehensive in-depth grasp of certain concepts, philosophies, ideas, art, or music) [**Do not include any aspect of your work or profession.**]

Now consider *you* as separate from K and U. Describe what you 'see'. Do not analyse or evaluate.

We acquire, gather knowledge such as facts and figures (facts and figures may strictly be considered as data or information rather than knowledge) about things all the time. However, do we really understand the knowledge that we gather. In addition do we attempt to gather knowledge about ourselves and if we have knowledge about ourselves do we attempt to understand this knowledge, and based on this understanding do we attempt to make any changes.

Consider how we gather knowledge nowadays – TV, internet, newspapers. Many people use knowledge gained from the internet to make decisions and to say 'things' based on their knowledge gained from the internet. Many do not have the skill or education to differentiate between accurate, verifiable information and persuasive, subjective opinion. And there are lots of opinions on the internet.

Many people know lots of things (facts, figures etc.) but understand little. Often we know little about ourselves and understand ourselves even less. We need to work on ourselves as much as we focus on projects at work. To work on your self means more than gathering knowledge about yourself. It means understanding yourself in totality – you and who you are and your relationships with your environment. It means understanding and applying acquired knowledge before acquiring more knowledge.

Let the mistakes of others become your best teacher. Actively look and listen and remember the mistakes of others.

Self-Observation (SO) (Please re-read the definition and the comments about SO in the introduction)

SO is to be aware of yourself:

Remember each second of each day

Remember those who do not have the luxuries that you experienced today – House, car, job, ….

Remember each second that you interact with anyone.

Remember each sensation, taste or texture of what you eat, drink or feel.

SO: when you are simultaneously acutely aware of yourself and acutely aware of what you are viewing or interacting with.

Identification and Fascination

When you interact with a person or persons or watch a film without being aware of yourself we could say that you are in a state of fascination.

That is, according to certain schools of thought, you are mentally, emotionally and spiritually asleep. You are in a state created by other individuals not one of your own making. You are not in nor do you have, your '**own**' state of mind

There is a strong tendency, an almost overriding pressure for people to lose themselves in sports, TV, TV reality shows. ????????

Control of your imagination, desires and material wants requires discrimination. Consider discrimination as taste, discernment or refinement. *Therefore, if you lack discrimination your senses (wants, desires) are uncontrolled and unmanageable.*

Consider SO as one way to develop discrimination.

SO is something that is done naturally – that is, inconspicuously. It is not something you discuss or talk about. It is something you practice/do continuously without talking about it.

It is also something that you do not discuss or analyse with family or friends.

SO is a state of mind – the more you practice the better you become at 'being' aware of who you are and of your actions and reactions.

SO is to be aware of both yourself and who or what you are looking at or listening to, without analysis or criticism of the situation or event or the people involved including yourself.

SO indirectly helps you control and eliminate negative reactions and thoughts irrespective of the circumstances and or people involved.

SO helps overcome the preoccupation with self, imagination and attachment to people or groups of people.

Always remember that your imagination can be the most pervasive and insidious constraint to your growth and development.

Walk and connect with trees and the sea. – Become the tree. Become part of the sea. View yourself on the shore from the sea (SO from a long distance).

Mental Prisons and Centres of Gravity

Are you a 'prisoner' of your:

    Emotions,

    Financial situation,

    Culture,

    Family, parents, peers,

    or

    ?,?

Compare your answers to the above questions to your answers to the questions below.

How do you react to situations, events, other people, sudden 'problems' or acute situations? Do your reactions (irrespective of the situation or event) *primarily* come from your:

    Emotions?

    Logic or Intellect?

    Instinct?

    or

    what you may consider or believe is your Intuition

[Instinct is not the same as intuition]

The (so called) Subconscious Mind

Do you use the phrase, "I can't do 'this' " or "I can't do 'that' "?

Change your thoughts and you change your future.

This is why SO and SR are considered important because (if practiced correctly) they automatically bring about change in thought and behaviour and therefore a change in your future

Provocation and Bitterness

SO also helps observe the emotional, financial and social 'problems' or 'issues' of family, friends, work associates and colleagues so that we can learn from the mistakes of others.

> *"Let your best teacher be the observation and the remembering of the decisions, actions and mistakes of other people or organizations."*

SO helps you become more perceptive of yourself, to what is happening around you and to how you have been unconsciously conditioned and influenced, in the past, by the actions and words of other people, groups or organisations.

SO will appear to make time slow down and will facilitate the exploration and discovery of your true self.

Do you continuously analyse or criticise the actions or behaviour of those around you or those you do not really know? If so, is it because you are disappointed with yourself or are you angry with yourself or someone else?

The many "Is" (within us) control us endlessly unless controlled and erased. – Many people seek to identity with something or someone. Observe people who use cars as a form of identity. Some people often get into debt over a car because image is an extremely important aspect of their lives. There are some individuals who will even spend more money on a car than on their own health and well-being.

Imagination, at times, may be the expression of irrational, negative emotions. For example, thoughts such as, "What if this happens?", "What if this goes wrong?"

I am not talking about being cautious or careful. We are talking about people who tend to use imagination to talk themselves or others out of doing something, or saying something without understanding the full picture and not understanding the consequences of their actions.

Omar Khayyam said, "There is a Door to which I found no Key: there was the veil through which I could not see."

Consider the veil as a combination of your conditioning and imagination and consider SO as one of a number of means to lift the veil and find the key. Even when found the Key can only be grasped by those with self-control and charity and compassion in their hearts.

Imagination, identification, association, negative thoughts, actions, behaviour, self-pity all contribute to the veil that restricts our vision to what often stares us in the face BUT is unseen.

We must at all times transform suffering into something positive – use suffering to SO. If you physically or mentally hurt keep Self Observing, SO, SO. Suffering can take many forms, some large some small. Create your own list.

Do not react to provocation – Stop, laugh to yourself and SO.

Laughter without SO will not help you, crying without SO will not help you. Consider SO as a critical means towards self-awareness.

Negativity

Always look for the source of, or the reasons for your negative thoughts, behaviour or actions. When did a specific type of reaction or pattern of behaviour first appear? If certain forms or types of negative behaviour keep occurring why do you keep letting them happen? It is only when you start to understand and thereby control and change or eliminate the 'source' of your negativity that you can change or modify the perceived nature of an event and eliminate or modify negative reactions or responses. It sounds a little long-winded but all you have to do is keep Self-Observing (SO).

Why do you continuously accept and condone your negative reactions to events and individuals? It may be because it is a 'soft option' and because of the effort it takes to look for the underlying reasons. If we do not make any effort to counter negativity in our lives it can continue and increase in frequency and intensity. Therefore it is important to aggressively and continuously counter each and every negative emotion and to eliminate all negative habits, feelings and phrases.

Every day, every hour there is a need to reject all forms of negative emotions, reactions or activities. Do not allow yourself to become negative - SO

Who gives you permission to be negative, antagonistic to others, or to criticize or blame other people?

Remember it is you (and you alone) who gives yourself permission to become negative or critical of others.

If you feel you are losing your temper immediately start counting to 10 slowly and SO.

"You can think anything you wish,
but you may not say anything you wish"
P. Ouspensky

A negative emotion, thought or action may appear 'small or unimportant' and of little consequence at the time and therefore you may feel or consider it not worth countering. However, it is often the small negatives that grow and intensify into large corrosive negative actions and thoughts.

An imagination out of control can create negative emotions or magnify negative emotions.

Transforming negative emotions is the process of turning the situation or feeling into one of personal understanding. For example, what is the source of this negative emotion (-E), why am I reacting in this way?

Our personal growth and transformation can be 'gauged" and assessed by the degree to which we stop expressing negative emotions and stop spontaneous negative reactions to situations or people we do not like (for various reasons) or disagree with. 'Disagreements' often arise over the most superficial and 'stupid' things.

Use every event or situation (no matter how small or trivial) during which negative emotions may arise to SO and transform.

Use every period of real or perceived suffering to SO.

ALWAYS BE AWARE OF THE TIME YOU WERE IN PAIN OR ILL AND APPRECIATE THE PRESENT WHEN YOU ARE NOT IN PAIN OR DISCOMFORT

The **culture** in which we are raised is usually the predominant influence that colours our vision, thoughts and actions.

Often "culture" is the largest obstacle to overcome in order to see 'objectively' and clearly. What does this mean? It means appreciating and understanding the *reasons* for the feelings and the actions of other individuals and groups.

Unnecessary talk hinders SO. Is the incessant, fast talker vain?

It is not necessary to live in a monastery, go on an expensive retreat, or have total silence to increase consciousness or SO. It may help but it will not produce 'industrial strength' benefits.

Basics: The basics of self-awareness, consciousness or any similar terminology involve more than the deconstruction, dismantling or obliteration of deep-rooted values, identities and related behaviour. It literally requires, for some, the rewiring or re-routing of neural paths to produce an entirely new way of thinking and acting based on new values and perceptions. This requires the **constant** practice of, for example, SO. We can consider that one of the aims of SO is to help you (automatically and in the background) reroute.

Consider Consciousness or Self-Awareness in relation to: Self Control and Self Discipline (which is much more than the elimination of Impatience); Charity, Compassion, and the Tolerance and Acceptance of others (Tolerance is of little value without Acceptance - We need to both Tolerate and Accept what is 'normal' to others although it may not be 'normal' to ourselves.); The elimination of: all forms of Impatience and Criticism, and the blaming of others.

How does SO help:

It helps dampen and eliminate deep-rooted negative attitudes and beliefs that result from past conditioning.

It helps a person become less critical and analytical of others. As you stop analysing the actions and behaviour of others you will no longer be disappointed with yourself (if this is the issue.)

It helps a person to become less frustrated in traffic, queues; stops a person lying to himself.

Stop blaming others (for anything and everything.) How often have you heard, "They did this or they did that…..."

When you blame others for an event, a situation, even your own behaviour it may result in further negative behaviour by yourself. When this happens you know you have not been practicing SO.

Speculation, rumour, assumptions based on the opinions of others may lead you astray. Always question unqualified opinions, statements, claims or declarations.

Suggestion:

As a student, when someone makes a statement or claim:

Always say, "Give me an example" and "Did you experience this 'example' or "did you hear this from someone" or "did you read this", "where did you read this"

This is not a very subtle approach and is in fact a brute force approach. Use selectively and <u>very gently (speak softy & slowly)</u>.

A real example is NOT something that was read in a book, seen in a film or related by the proverbial and ubiquitous unseen 'They'. Remember, in the *beginning of your journey* always ask, "Who are they". As you progress you will stop asking.

It is when you stop asking questions because you have received the answer before the person speaks that you will know that you are starting to make progress. However, it is only when you have the negative aspect of your imagination under control and Self-Observation has become part of the fabric of your life that this phenomenon may, over time, slowly start to emerge. It is also not something that you must think about or constantly expect to happen.

Observe and remember when and in what circumstances you:

Are overly dissatisfied or disappointed with something or someone, or disappointed because you did not receive 'something' that you expected, or someone did not take notice of you (when you wanted or expected them to take notice.)

Compete with someone at work or in class for no real reason.

Feel sorry for yourself, depreciate yourself in front of others or always act the underdog in front of others.

Let your imagination run wild. What if this happens., What if someone… 'What ifs' are important in day to day life but NOT when an overly active imagination is activated by assumptions based on or initiated by unfounded opinion, rumour or innuendo, or someone else's assumptions.

Overly identify or become fascinated with someone, a team, a thing, a place, a particular type of behaviour, or particular way of speaking or dressing.

Observe these daily events and thoughts and remember (but do not analyse) which centre (logic, intellectual or emotional centre etc.), is in control in each situation.

Remember your emotions and which specific reflexes, actions or words dominated in the above situations.

More Imagination and Identification

Imagination and Identification with people are things which reduce our ability to SO

Identification is a ?

Imagination can be an acute manifestation of a ?

Often we are totally unaware of the small simple things that take place around us because our imagination continuously vies for our attention. We often look for the negative and look for what may or could go wrong.

This does not imply that we must be overly optimistic and unrealistic in our thoughts or actions.

Identification can be considered a transfer of negative attributes to another.

Consideration and forgiveness of others for their mistakes is a critical part of experiencing our essence. Make things happen.

Consider

The Frog in warm water

The 'lucky' golf player.

When you observe things try and mentally group or classify what you observe or where they come from – from your intellect or logic, emotions, instinct, or from intuition. Only observe and classify, do not try to analyse or 'think' about why or how etc. In the beginning remember to observe and only observe. Change takes time.

As you observe (if done properly) you will notice how your actions and thought patterns change (over time) – you may even do the opposite to what you set out to do. New patterns may start to appear. "You", may start to appear. From the small details and changes the whole may start to appear

Understanding requires experience. Experience comes from an increase in knowledge (knowing what to do) and the simultaneous and effective application of that knowledge. That is, an increase in self-awareness and Self.

Consider self-awareness to include consistency of actions. That is, an absence of contradictory actions or thought over time.

Note:

Contradictory actions do not necessarily mean you are weak or inconsistent. Changed circumstances may require a change of mind. Do not resist change where appropriate. People often make the mistake of resisting change because they feel that they will 'lose face' or look foolish.

And if all others accepted the lie which the Party imposed

if all records told the same tale

then the lie passed into history and became truth.

"1984"

by George Orwell,

"We are here only to contend with ourselves. So thank others who provide you with the opportunity for doing so"

G. I. G.

HEALING
QUANTUM
SPIRITUAL
COSMOLOGICAL

What's in a Word?

Healing

> For this discussion "healing" means the restoration of a sense of wholeness as in holism or awareness as in Self
>
> Healing involves both a sense of oneness of mind and body but also a sense of oneness or wholeness with the universe. The eradication of any disease or physical condition may or may not be associated with healing.
>
> Many people consider that healing is related to spirituality and prayer. J. B. Rhine, the founder of modern parapsychology, believes that, for example, intercessory prayer is related to psychokinesis. That is, the mind affecting matter.

Quantum (a much misused term and totally overused word)

> According to quantum laws it is not possible to predict the future with certainty only the probability that things will happen. That is, outcomes cannot be predicted. Only the odds that things will turn out one way or another can be predicted.

Entanglement and Non-Locality

> Quantum mechanics implies that something you do over here can be instantaneously linked to something happening over there, regardless of distance. That is, spatial separation does not imply physical independence (that is, non-locality).
>
> That is, two objects (although far apart) are considered as a single entity because they do not "have a fully independent existence."

Spirituality (consider the conflict between physicists and non-physicists: non-locality vis-à-vis prayer)

"Spiritual"- Consider the term in relation to 'Brahman, ..the Absolute which transcends space, time and causality.'; 'the innate Wisdom resident in the depth of all consciousness.' The Absolute may be referred to as God, Allah or whatever term is appropriate to you.

> *"Natural forces within us are the true healers of disease"*
> Hippocrates, c 460-377 BC

> *"Each celestial body, in fact each and every atom, produces a particular sound on account of its movement, its rhythm or vibration. All these sounds and vibrations form a universal harmony in which each element, while having its own function and character contributes to the whole."*
> Pythagoras

Good, Evil and the Soul

The concept of evil (or good) differs from person to person and from culture to culture.

It is also subjective in that for one person 'evil is everything that is opposed to his desires or interests or to his conception of good'.

Therefore one group of men may kill or bomb another group in the interests of 'good' because the other is 'evil' or 'bad'.

How many men consider everything, which does not match their definition of good, to be evil? It makes for a dangerous world.

The man with fixed, rigid ideas offers no compromises nor entertains dialogue in any form. His manner quickly turns belligerent when opposed and he always considers himself to be 'right'.

In some cultures 'good' and 'evil' are considered part and parcel of morality. What is morality? How many crimes have been committed in the name of morality? Is it 'ok' to kill a person because he is considered 'evil' or is part of an 'evil' group.

According to Bertrand Russell, "It would appear that knowledge concerning the universe as a whole is <u>not</u> to be obtained by metaphysics, and that the supposed proofs, that in virtue of the laws of logic, such and such things must exist and such and such others cannot, are not capable of surviving a critical scrutiny"

An 'only' logical or local mind is linear and therefore restrictive. Adopting the attitude 'anything is possible' has led to experiments in nonlocal interactions that show that the past is not fixed but can alter according to present conditions and that the effects of empathic bonding transcend space and time.

Bertrand Russell defines the human soul as "a battleground of two natures, the one particular, finite, self-centred, the other universal, infinite, and impartial."

Consider the description of finite man as a person who may create division and strife in his surroundings. He considers only himself and the views and thoughts of others are of little consequence. He may use phrases such as 'You are for us or against us" He may also pit one person against another or one group of people against another group in order to achieve his own aims.

Therefore, in this context, the finite man may be considered as destructive in that he is a person who is a destroyer of all who do not conform to his wants and ideals. He may also be devious and manipulative and will say and do 'whatever it takes' to get what he wants. He may depict the classic traits of many dictators past and present. These traits may (obviously) not be restricted to dictators.

Words similar to 'you are for me or against me' appear in the Christian Bible. The finite man may translate the phrase literally whereas the infinite man will use an esoteric translation.

Let us define or consider the infinite man as the man of compassion and sharing on the basis that he has many views, and views the universe through not only his eyes but through the 'eyes' of all others, including animals.

Whatever it takes attitude...

Winning (in its various forms) is not all about physical fitness, numbers or money. The belief that you can achieve something increases the possibility of success. However, if you believe you cannot achieve that something it decreases the possibility of success and often means that you do not even attempt what may be possible, and what may change your life for the better. Winning is very much about attitude and behaviour.

However, what is becoming ubiquitous is the attitude of "win – whatever it takes". That is, win even if it means cheating, lying, stealing, fraud, etc. Respect for the traditions and values of others is now at an all-time low in the world.

In all aspects of life let us consider two beliefs. Belief in "Self" and belief in "Anything is Possible". However, these two values often need to be instilled and reinforced over and over in a person until it becomes part and parcel of his or her 'make-up'. However, balance is critical. The aim is to instil confidence, not to create a super ego. Humility which we discuss later is of equal importance.

Prayer and meditation are also part and parcel of 'Self" and "Anything is Possible." For example, clinical experiments to test the efficiency of intercessory prayer for healing have proved that prayer is effective. Not that some people need to be convinced. Daily prayer, meditation or a daily mantra are emotional 'counters' or counter-balances to the stresses that one may experience during the day.

Remember, it requires practice, practice, practice and more practice to bring about positive change in your life. There are no shortcuts. It is a matter of daily practice. Even when you think or feel you have achieved a higher level of consciousness you may suddenly find that you have to start over again. In the words of Collins, based on the work of Ouspensky "They realized that on the way to development true knowledge must first be acquired and then abandoned. That exactly what makes possible the opening of one door may make impossible the opening of the next."

William James wrote "Often enough our faith beforehand in an uncertified result is the only thing that makes the result come true." Having faith in oneself during difficult or dangerous circumstances is critical to managing or surviving those circumstances.

Time

Consider time as the only thing that you possess. Therefore, how you use that time to your best advantage is *your* decision.

Time is not the same for everyone. Compare a 6 year-old child's perception of time to a 60 year-old person's perception of time and an 80 year-old person's perception of time. As we get older, for some, time appears to speed up. This perception of time is *not* related to, and is separate from, the rate and pace of life compared to say 30 or more years ago.

Consider everything that happens today and every day from now on as the culmination of your life. That is, experience every nuance of every second and simultaneously do whatever you do to the best of your ability and with extreme care and attention, and at the same time treat everyone you meet with consideration and compassion. A 'tall- order' for some - a normal day for others.

In some ancient and modern cultures and groups the word 'time' (in general terms) did not and still does not exist. These groups tend to live longer, healthier and more contented lives when compared to cultures or groups who have a fixation on 'time' and who are controlled by the concept of time (when to eat, when to work….). An interesting documentary a few years ago (I believe it was the BBC) showed that in a few small villages in Sicily, the word 'time' did not exist in their local dialect. Within these groups it was also common to find people of 100 years of age or more, a number of whom were still physically active.

We could say that they ignore 'time'. However, they follow or followed the course of the sun, the moon and the tides. To a fisherman of 1000 years ago only the tides were important irrespective of the 'time' that they occurred.

Time is relative (to what and to whom – these are usually important qualifiers). To men of the same age (in a normal state) time is the 'same' because their metabolic rates are the same.

Consider the concept of time as man-made.

Suffering and Emotions

Whenever you experience an emotional or mental upheaval use that event or situation to progress emotionally, intellectually and spiritually. You may consider or view the nature of the event or situation as negative or positive, it makes no difference. If you consider the event or situation as negative it is critical that you take advantage of it and use it as a learning experience. [SO is the rule at all times]

When a stressful event arises, at work or at home, it may be difficult to follow and apply everything that you have read in this book, or discussed or even practiced in a group. Therefore, practice the following exercise as often as you can. The following is only a suggestion and not advice. You can develop different exercises of your own.

Sit in front of an arrangement of flowers or fruit and consider all aspects of the objects in front of you:

Smell, texture, colour, shape, images or memories that are evoked. Consider all these things simultaneously while at the same time remaining aware of yourself (that is, your posture, your breathing, your physical sensations and your thoughts, your position in relation to the objects in front of you, your relationship to those objects.) Place yourself in a relaxed state while you experience awareness of yourself and the objects in front of you.

When you are in an emotional situation consider all the processes and individuals involved and observe both the situation and yourself. Do not be panicked into making any rash decisions or statements.

Time, for many people, seems to slow down and things seem to happen in slow motion, even stop, when they are faced with a sudden, life or death situation.

Suffering and Negative Emotions

Examples of negative emotions are: Irritability, impatience, anger, fear, self-pity, jealousy, greed, hatred, etc.

Who is responsible for these negative emotions? The answer is 'you'. Not the events (real or perceived) that you may think of or blame as the initiators of these feelings or reactions.

No amount of watching the latest DVD or listening to the latest CD or reading the latest book about consciousness or being in the present will eliminate these feelings or reactions to various stimuli. It takes daily practice during everyday activities.

The direction, depth and nature of our thoughts have a direct impact on our physical body. Let us say that harmonising thoughts produce harmonising energy or information and disruptive thoughts will produce disruptive energy or information.

Disruptive energy/information disrupts the normal or good patterns of vibrations in and around our bodies and results in disease or organ malfunction. Emotions, anger, and fear often suppressed and harboured for years are often cited as the cause of ill-health or contributing to ill-health.

Often for many individuals the root cause of disruptive thoughts is another person. Again, very often it may turn out to be a family member. In order to create and maintain harmonizing thoughts, in order to dampen and then eliminate the disruptive energy, one has to first forgive and forget.

Without forgiveness the process is flawed and will fail. **Why, because it is a critical factor in human physiological and mental harmony. Why, again? Because, if the original disruptive event is still present in the background, it can reappear at any time to disrupt current events.**

In order to create and maintain harmonising thoughts all emotional connections with the person or persons who were the initial, and I stress, the initial creators of the problem must be severed. Visualize the breaking of those connections and simultaneously send love and forgiveness. This requires effort and practice.

The Buddha said that attachment to material things or possessions is the basis of all man's pain or suffering or sorrow. However, it appears Buddhism is now becoming main stream – numerous adverts for seminars, workshops on Buddhism or related topics etc.

Consider the following:

1.

Continual judgement and criticism of others often goes hand in hand with resentment and frustration.

Fear, judgement, criticism and unresolved personal or emotional conflicts are the great human destroyers of self. Arrogance, a totally different element, is the great destroyer of others.

Examine your daily life and remember when and where you criticise other people and remember any resentment or frustration that may arise when this happens. Do not try to analyse the situation or the factors or people surrounding the situation. Simply observe, observe and observe.

2.

Fear of disease, death or loss.

Fear of loss, disease, death or injury, continuous worry or anxiety may all contribute to a slow degradation of human health both physically and mentally. Fear of material loss in particular may lead to a slow degradation of a society that is devoid of morality or values. This type of society often displays a false image of morality and displays great indignation when criticised.

Fears of disease, death or loss are subtle and are similar to low, continuous back-ground noise. Always present but not creating or resulting in any acute symptoms. However, its impact is insidious and far reaching. You get used to the noise and it stops registering as something abnormal and not natural.

When you have a critical or important decision to make consider the following suggestion:

Observe yourself during the time in which you have to make the decision. Or, if it is not possible or the activity is fast and complex simply proceed as normal and then rerun the activity in your mind and observe what happened and how you reacted.

Simply observe, observe and observe during the activity or when you rerun it in your mind.

3.

Inner concern (or lack of inner concern) resulting from what may be considered inappropriate social behaviour.

The attitude of 'whatever it takes'. Lie, cheat, deceive, etc. – do whatever it takes to win or get what you want is displayed endlessly on TV and in films. Therefore, many viewers may adopt the attitude 'that's life'.

Is TV the reason why such behaviour also appears to be accepted by many people? Also, is this the reason that such behaviour does not cause any concern or further thought?

However, again monitor yourself and look for what you may consider any sudden or chronic tension in life. Again, only observe and look for a cause or origin even if it may have occurred months or years ago. Do not attempt to analyse it in any way. Continue to observe yourself during your daily activities.

4.

Anger

Observe yourself and monitor any feelings of what you may consider anger. Look into your past and try to identity any period of your life where you may have experienced intense anger for whatever reason. Decide whether that anger was resolved or not.

Speed and Haste

The name of the game today is speed – faster is better.

People eat and drink in cars to save time. There are drive through restaurants, drive through pharmacies – the list goes on.

How   do   we   slow   down?

We slow down by realizing that the next second, the next moment, is no greater or more important than the present moment. Many people may argue or disagree.

Crisis, emotional or physical shocks or upheavals provide opportunities to SO and learn from the experience. We could say that it is only when you learn from an experience that you were really 'present' during the experience.

However, do not make the present into something it is **not**. Do **not** assume it is something special or different. Watch your imagination at all times. Is it leading you astray?

Who are You?

1.

Is your face to the world your name, your training or education, your title or job title? Or is it what you own or possess? Or is it the information, education in your head or the professional skill that you possess?

Apart from your name and what you have accumulated in your head, who are you?

What do you represent? Who do you represent?

Is it your title, your car, your house etc. What if you do not possess large assets or a fancy title? How do you judge, describe or assess a person?

2.

When we break with our past which represents our conditioned thought and patterns of behaviour we have the opportunity and ability to become more creative. By creativity I mean the communication and the expression of our true Self and the ability to help others.

Therefore, in this context creative means to become **self-sufficient**. That is, *not* to give up our inherent skills.

Scenario: Consider a country where, for example, hawkers along the side of the road make small trinkets to sell to tourists. These trinkets came in the shape of bicycles, animals or flowers etc. They used to be made from old or used pieces of thin wire and old beer and soft-drinks cans. The hawker obtained the materials and produced his own goods often at the place where he sold his goods.

They were originally crude but original and unique and therefore much desired. Also, as previously mentioned, the hawker was usually the collector of the used, raw material, the designer of the product, and the manufacturer and the seller of his product.

Now, consider the following scenario where logic and rationality have robbed them of these skills and therefore the ability to express themselves, support themselves and to be creative. How and why could this happen?

We could debate that it is because an educated and therefore logical and rational mind has seen an opportunity to make money. There is nothing wrong with making money or helping others make money. However, what are the long term implications for all the people who are impressed by rational and logical thoughts without understanding the long term implications. Therefore, in this scenario you notice that many of the items sold along the road are now extremely well made and uniform.

You could be buying the item off-the-shelf in some department store. Why, because many if not most of the items are now made in small 'mass assembly' shops. The owner or owners of these shops now sell to the hawker who is now simply a salesman. Instead of being creative and in a simple sense master of his own destiny he simply becomes a cog in a much bigger wheel. Progress some may say.

However, without practice the previous craftsman and salesman is now only a salesman who may lose his artistic skills. Also, is the craftsman who originally sold his own products, but may now work in a manufacturing shop, happy and satisfied, and will he continue to be as creative as before?

Evaluate the above scenario and put your thoughts down on paper.

3.

We create our world each and every second through our thoughts, actions and words. If we are the creators of our world we can therefore shape our world according to how we would like to interact with those around us.

Two of the things that influence us every day are the images and information that we receive through the media, especially television.

Do you feel that mental, emotional interference or disturbances in the form of TV news and advertising can disrupt peaceful and harmonious thought flows and leave one with anxiety or dissatisfaction? Consider and observe carefully.

AWARENESS: (An optional exercise)

Find a quiet, secluded place free of phones or disturbances. Sit, stand, or lie in a position that gives your body some freedom to move. Relax and breathe normally but as deeply and slowly as possible remaining relaxed at all times.

During this period do not think about family, friends, cats, dogs, work etc. Simply, feel the sensation (on your skin) over your entire body. Relax and be aware of your body and the energy around it. If you feel or perceive that your body wants to move in some way do not fight or resist the sensation – just feel and experience this sensation and slowly allow your body to move in the direction indicated by the sensation.

For example, if at any time you feel you need to move around the room or you feel the need to dance, wave your arms, or shake your legs follow those feelings as long as they bring no harm to yourself.

If during this period any images or ideas appear mentally explore those images or ideas and allow them to expand and dominate your thoughts. If images or ideas arise consider if they give meaning or understanding to the movements or sensations you are experiencing?

What do these images or sensations mean to you? Allow your intuition to answer not your logical, rational mind.

While this is happening if you feel any emotions or physical symptoms related to your health, let them flow and make a mental note of them. They could be a precursor or subtle warning that you should take greater care health wise or that you adopt some sort of prevention regime.

Finally, after noting the possible meaning of these images or sensations go back to your movements and ask your body what does this all mean?

Judgement and Criticism

Consider the following:

1. Continual judgement and criticism

If you are in a life or death situation where time is of the essence every second is critical.

If you are not in a life or death situation consider the current moment as no more important than the next. Therefore there is no real hurry. Even if speed is considered or perceived as important but in reality is not really important this possible approach will help you to hurry in a relaxed state rather than in an agitated state.

Road signs warn motorists that "Speed kills". Performing tasks in an agitated and hurried state has detrimental effects on the body and can also result in death where heavy machinery is involved.

Some of the things we are going to look at today are many practical daily mental exercises and approaches to life that can and will help you transform existing negative emotions and habits. These exercises and approaches are meant to be undertaken during your normal day. It is not necessary to go on a retreat or sit on top of a mountain or enter a monastery to achieve results. Emotions or thoughts transformed under ideal conditions are often not as strong or robust as those forged under not so ideal conditions.

The key is practice, practice and more practice. It is a philosophy, a philosophy of life that includes nothing new and no secrets in the esoteric sense. Illusions, subtle suggestions and perceptions create secrets.

Who are We?

We are all conditioned, in many ways, *even in the womb*, by many events, processes, people and organizations. Let us take a very quick look at the events, people and organizations that influence us from birth.

First of all - who are we? What are we?

Apart from TV, internet, newspapers or magazines what or who influences us on a daily basis? Make separate lists of the people, events and organisations or groups that you consider have had a positive influence on your life. Make a second set of lists of the people, events and organizations or groups that you consider have had a negative influence on your life.

Do you consider many people to be similar to robots or machines, controlled by the programs in their minds that have been created by the people and organizations described in the definition of 'conditioning'?

There are many individuals from all walks of life who have over the years always marched according to their own drum beat. Many we have never heard of and will never hear of. Again, there are many reasons for not hearing about them which will be discussed at a later date.

However, their drum beat includes compassion, respect and concern for others and their environment.

We could say that the conditioning described in the above models puts many people in a controlled mental state or conditioned consciousness where certain words, images or views, due to past suggestions and conditioning, will trigger physical, verbal or emotional reactions. Our view of ourselves and of the world is often based on our past conditioning.

Numerous schools of thought say that essentially we go through life in a hypnotized or semi-drugged state – that we can be directed and influenced by a few key words or phrases - that it is easy for those who know the key words and phrases to direct or influence our thoughts and actions, especially in a world dominated by TV and the internet. Obviously, it is not necessary for these individuals to know each and every one of us. A few words or pictures and our conditioned mental programs kick-in and take control.

Are you conscious at all levels?

Radical transformation from conditioned consciousness to enlightened consciousness requires daily step by step effort. It involves, among other things, concern for the welfare of people you do not know and wanting to help them, in addition to empathising with and showing respect to people you may not have considered before.

The subtle and not so subtle feelings that may emerge during this process need to be observed continuously. Only observation of the feelings and any actions or reactions (created by these feelings) is required. It is critical that no analysis of the feelings or actions takes place. The reason why will be explained later.

Daily Guide – Attitude

Learn and practice not to take things personally at any time.

Do not make assumptions about what may or may not have happened in the *past* (with respect to people, places or things)

Do not make assumptions about what may or may not happen in the *future* (with respect to people, places or things)

Duality, Non-Duality and Polarisation

Historically, (as a generalisation) certain western minds have tended, to a certain degree, to think in dualistic terms. Take polarity for example, "You are for or against us" – George Bush. In this instance this phrase is used or viewed in a literal sense. [However, when viewed from an esoteric perspective, as opposed to the literal interpretation, this phrase has an alternative or different meaning.]

From a literal perspective the phrase implies that if you are not 'for us' you are our enemy. That is, polarity tends to view things, look at things, in life from a very black or white perspective. That is, order versus chaos, good versus evil, truth or lies, me or you, I am 'right' therefore you are 'wrong', 'matter' versus 'spirit', active versus passive, and finally conscious versus unconscious.

Therefore let us consider *dualism* as a habit of thought or as a particular 'state of mind'. Many people require or need clear-cut solutions to problems and unambiguous understanding of events or processes. It creates, in some minds, order and a feeling of security. However, polarity (strictly enforced) can give rise to conflict and force. Polarity can cause conflict within a family and just as easily result in war between nations.

Many people still think in strictly dualistic terms (where things are mutually exclusive) and do not consider or will not consider, for various reasons, alternative approaches or alternative ways of thinking and making decisions.

Let us therefore define non-duality as a way of thinking that does not create force, conflict or friction.

Let us also define non-duality as the <u>acceptance</u> of the many divisions that we see in everyday life and those that we create in our own lives as <u>mental or emotional divisions</u>.

Let us consider that the non-dualistic mind, for want of a better word, does not use western logic or reasoning to arrive at a conclusion or decision. Let us also consider that intuition is an integral aspect of the non-dualistic mind but not intuition that harbours doubts or conditioning or opinions and subtle interference of others. It is intuition from the pure essence of the body and soul. It may also come from an awareness and appreciation of all things living and what some may consider non-living things.

The non-dualistic mind or for that matter the purely intuitive mind does not, in fact cannot, conform to so called western values, rules, logic or laws. Why? Because such laws or logic are not applied equally to all men. Why you may ask. Because all men are not viewed as equal under such laws. Culture, social status, money, political connections easily bend such laws.

However, you may say, "This happens in all countries not only so called Western countries." Remember, many Eastern countries are becoming very 'Westernised" and their ethnic values and customs corrupted, rightly or wrongly.

Consider the following experience of talking to and treating (health wise) 'street people' in Pune, India. The overwhelming impression was that the sole interest of many of these people was "tell me what I can do to keep healthy". They were interested in what physical exercise to do and what to eat. Yes, what to eat even though they were living on the street. They realised that as long as they kept healthy they could look after themselves. They did not expect the government to look after them or support them. That is, they took full responsibility for themselves.

What is permitted in one country may be considered illegal in another. Which country is 'right'? Who has the right to say "I" am right and you are wrong.

Let us consider non-dualism to be about perceiving, appreciating, seeing relationships and connections which we could not see or appreciate before, and which result from an awareness that is not based on western style logic but one which comes about from living, daily, minute by minute, according to a philosophy of universal laws.

Many events in life ranging from sports games to social events only begin because a certain rule or protocol has been followed. Most people choose to abide by these fixed rules. That is, they accept these rules as fixed and not negotiable. Always remember to consider whether man-made limitations or self-limiting rules are truly applicable to a situation and if they make you feel uncomfortable in any way. The universe has little time for man's self-limiting rules which have been created and imposed by individuals or groups and which only serve the creators of the rules.

What about your neighbour?

Today, treat *everyone* that you meet as you would like to be treated.

You have got nothing to lose.

Aspects of Healing

A modern version of Hamlet's quote could read "We *think* we know what or who we are, and we do not work enough at what we may be"

Perspectives on healing from Dr E Loomis:

Four essentials in the healing process:

You must want to be healed.

You must have faith that you can be healed.

You must ask for forgiveness of every one you have injured in some way.

You must change your life and reduce any emphasis or focus you have on the material aspects of your life.

Indian Medicine Man

Dr E Loomis considers illness or dis-ease, no matter how 'unwell' a person may feel, as an opportunity to reflect on the following:

Why did the illness appear at a particular time.

Are there particular lessons to be learnt from the illness or disease?

He also says that you should study and think slowly and carefully about the above statements in relation to yourself and any past or present illness. Your present state of health is significantly related to your past and present attitudes and behaviour.

The seminars and workshops, associated with this book, encompass a wide variety of subjects that range from consciousness, intuition, sound and light (related to consciousness and healing), biofeedback, quantum entanglement, and bio-electromagnetic healing, to radionics. Attendance of the workshop requires no special skills or education. The only prerequisite is an open mind and the desire to learn.

According to G Gurdjieff for a man to truly understand himself he must first rid himself of what may be called 'false conceptions' or 'false assumptions' about himself. Progress is not about landing a man on the moon, how many houses you possess or how much money you make. Let us define progress as the process of knowing and understanding yourself and the use of this knowledge for the development of your 'soul' or any *similar* term that is appropriate to your culture, background or language. We will discuss more at a later stage.

'Understanding' grows only with the growth of 'being'. Growth of 'being' comes from self-observation and self-remembering. Therefore, any 'feelings of loneliness or detachment' are always opportunities for SO.

There is more to 'self-observation' and 'self-remembering' than one normally thinks and the effectiveness of both of these practices is often underestimated.

The Way to Liberation is said to be, "Know thyself"

Historically, the phrase "Know yourself" is generally attributed to Socrates. However, it is also said to be the basis of many ancient philosophies and religions. To know one-self a person needs to study one-self. This again involves 'self-observation' and 'self-remembering', not a study that involves any detailed analysis and or conclusions. It also involves what may be termed 'starting from the beginning'. That is, we need to unlearn a few of the bad habits and thoughts that we have picked up along the way. This is where SO and SR come into play. SO and SR form a part of the way to get back to the beginning.

However, we must be careful when using this phrase and in defining the processes involved in our search for self because 'Self' is another term, similar to consciousness, which is ambiguous and often *misleading*. Also, as mentioned many times, unlearning often needs to take place before searching can begin.

Consider your physical body as an organism that responds to external stimuli (physical and non-physical [words, pictures, views etc.]). Consider your brain and spinal cord as the mechanism, in this organism, that receives and transmits these external stimuli to other parts of the organism. Also consider the brain and the spinal cord as the controlling mechanism of your body.

Consider your brain as your mind. Therefore, your mind is a mechanism that's function is to think. It thinks very quickly and carefully because it keeps your body functioning even when 'you' attack and abuse your body. There are certain occasions when your body might and does attack itself but normally it does not.

Even when you abuse your body your mind protects your body. Why, because one of its functions is to keep you in homeostasis which means it keeps your body in a state of physiological balance, which simply means it keeps your body well-tuned.

Your mind does this perfectly well without your interference. Therefore, we must be out of our minds if we interfere with this mind of ours. In fact most of the time, I am sure, it would prefer us to leave it alone. If we are not physically abusing it (via the abuse of our body) we also send it strange messages. Mind I want a 4-wheel drive; mind I want a bigger house. Your mind is busy keeping you alive and doing some very complicated stuff and all you are doing is distracting it with a 4-wheel drive and a bigger house.

So who is this person, where does he come from and where does he live? Who trained him? Who educated him? Where do all his whims and wishes come from?

Let us call him 'Will'. How does "Will' function when compared to mind.

Does he function based on **logic**?

Does he function based on **emotions**?

Does he function based on **intuition**?

Does he function based on **built-in programs that he was born with?**

Does he function based on **imagination – the dark side?**

Now consider your 'Will' compared to your 'Mind'.

[A person's imagination can create wonderful architecture or art. However, it can also lead us astray]

Many of us constantly react to our emotions and in turn, our imagination, which often takes control of our minds for short or long periods. Our imagination may sow a seed that controls us indirectly and can take us in directions that we had no intention of going, and in doing so can waste months or years.

Our imagination therefore acts against our best interest by getting us to act or think about what may happen in the future or to waste energy about something that happened in the past. If we consider all aspects of our past conditioning (parents, school, government, culture,..) we may begin to see that we often do not act in our own long-term best interests.

Remember, no one else can experience what you feel or experience. A person may 'think' or actually believe that he or she can feel or experience what another person feels, but do you believe it is possible? In rare cases let us say 'yes', and further let us say it involves extremely rare individuals who can do so.

The road towards 'Knowing yourself' begins with experiencing (feeling) and understanding the emotions that you go through minute by minute, and knowing where those emotions come from. Only then can you move to the next level of Consciousness. (Consciousness is defined (in the English language) in many ways and is simply a word of convenience as you will understand as you progress) As with everything else in this book, recognizing and understanding the origins and strength of these emotions requires practice, practice and more practice.

Our emotions may be influenced by our physical bodies because the body may be dominated by certain physical appetites. These emotions create thoughts and desires which can be amplified or modified by our imagination. If we have an imagination that is a little over active and a body that dominates our emotions we then simply become robots under the control of our imagination. In this situation we are merely robots or machines obeying the ever changing whims of our imagination and body. We are no longer in control.

It is only when we start to dominate our physical body and eliminate the negative influences of our imagination that we start to become aware of who we are and no longer react mechanically to external influences. We may begin to experience short periods of what may be termed mindfulness, awakening, self-awareness or consciousness etc. The aim is to achieve intense or total awareness of our actions and thoughts. It is only when we have full control over our thoughts and actions and have no (conditioned) feelings about the past or future that we can start to become aware or conscious.

We feed off our experiences and impressions and create our perception of the world. However, it is often a perception that is distorted or not real due to the fact that we have been severely conditioned by our past history.

We should aim to reach a point where, when we require our imagination to work, it responds to our thoughts or requests rather than reacting to its own old programs which can result in uncontrollable emotions and sensations. We need to control it so that we can develop new sensations and perspectives.

This includes the continuous practice of the development of the skill to observe in parallel how your emotions, intellect, education or instincts drive or run your daily activities. Only after extensive observation can you begin to take action to make any positive changes or make any form of analysis. Any form of analysis during the process of observation will actually hinder and destroy the observation process. The longer you observe, and only observe, the 'more' automatically the changes take place. That is, the process of the continuous observation of self slowly initiates a parallel process that not only modifies 'negative' behaviour but also slowly brings about the very early rays of self-awareness.

Metanoia - The Art of Transmutation

There are various techniques to show you the overriding or driving element in your life – your emotions, your logic or intellect or your instincts, and the relationships between those elements. However, although there may appear to be an overriding element it must be clearly understood that under certain circumstances or during certain situations *another* element may suddenly become dominant.

This journey also involves ridding oneself of ingrained prejudices, conditioned ways of reacting to people and situations, and most important, recognizing when and how you fool or deceive yourself. This requires a trust in yourself and a belief in what you intend to achieve which, when combined with the exercises described in this book, will create an environment in which different and advancing cycles of opportunities will appear and which you will need to recognize and take advantage of.

This journey requires continuous effort in all aspects of our daily life. However, although it may be physically or mentally demanding or tiring it should be a calm and relaxed effort, not a hand clenching, teeth gritting effort. Therefore, effort is not quite the right word. This effort becomes relaxed and calm when we maintain a "clear mind" and a clear and precise inner purpose (which at times may be indefinable and which may 'change' along the way – as strange as it may sound). It is a natural and inherent desire, and inner purpose (not overtly displayed) that will give us the energy and drive to progress along the way.

We periodically need physical or emotional difficulties to grow and develop. You may laugh and say, "I have enough stress in my life on an hourly basis so do not talk about the need for more problems."

Consider self-observation and self-remembering, combined with learning *from* our reaction to difficult situations, as activities that may contribute to growth and development. Growth may also be considered dependent upon the knowledge and skills used in a particular situation to transform consciousness.

Transmutation or transformation comes from what may be termed "disconnection from conditioned reality". That is, when you can simultaneously observe yourself now and in the past and take full cognizance of how you reacted and may still react to people and situations based on how and what you were taught to think in the past.

Real transformation often requires intense effort both physical and mental.

Sitting on top of a mountain and meditating may be fine for some but we cannot all sit on top of a mountain, attend endless weekend retreats or sit in the quiet of a monastery and contemplate the universe. We need to achieve inner peace no matter what the environment. Most of us, if we were in a safe environment and provided with permanent shelter and food, would also have a certain amount of inner peace.

Intense effort, particularly a combination of physical and mental effort creates a certain type of energy which is needed for self-transformation. Self-observation and the elimination of negative thoughts during the creation of this energy or information contributes towards self-transformation.

We need tools that help us in our daily life to achieve inner peace while there is chaos around us.

In the beginning we talked about personality and essence. In the modern sense (where a 'whatever it takes to win' attitude exists – lie, cheat, steal) or in the scientific sense - essence may be considered naïve or even childlike because it is not critical of others or influenced by logic. When a person's essence begins to dominate he or she may react or respond to family or friends in ways which may surprise or even annoy them because (now) that person does not conform, act or think in a way that conforms to their (family or friend) needs or wants. Why, because essence does not react to language, that is, the language, rules and conditioning of another person. [or persons who may be involved.]

Consider essence and personality as residing in different parts of the brain. Loosely speaking we can say that personality resides in the left brain and essence in the right brain. The right brain is also considered as possessing untapped sources of energy.

Suggestion:

For example, when you become tired after effort absorb yourself in something that 'takes you out of yourself'. That is, listen to some classical music, if you like classical music, and totally absorb yourself in the music. Suddenly you will experience energy you did not seem to have before.

Love your work whatever it may be, even sweeping the street. The more you love what you do the greater the energy you seem to have.

Metanoia - The Art of Transmutation

Let us define "Personality' (see definition) as something that tends to overreact, and is disposed to gloom and depression. It tends to overreact and is distrustful even of itself. When we act in an idiotic manner we could say that it is the 'fool' in us who is in temporary control of our personality.

Our personality has no time to talk or express itself when we work very hard at physical labour. It can be said that when our physical body is tired after hard physical labour it relaxes and the dominance or power of our personality is reduced. That is, it takes a back seat. When the body is tired and personality takes a back seat it allows essence to dominate or come to the fore. Therefore it is possible to become absorbed and "as one" with mental or emotional activities. There is no influence from personality (be it the fool or the dictator, or the ?) that contaminates or influences the situation. Suddenly when essence dominates outcomes (decisions or reactions) are very different from what may be the 'norm'. Why?

Because suddenly a person may feel that intuition 'kicks in' when essence dominates and is not over-ridden by logic or rationality.

Therefore, even when you are tired and you feel it is time to stop or give up push yourself a little further (without harming yourself) and see what "comes to mind". Does anger or resentment fade away? Do you suddenly find yourself with more energy?

How much physical, real physical work, do you put in during a week? I am not talking about sport, walking or cycling. Why do you think traditional farmers and fishermen (before automation and depth finders) could predict the weather, or 'knew' they would have a good crop or catch?

Some writers say that our left brain, which we will (for the time being) call our intellect, has a tendency to wear tinted glasses which keeps us hypnotised or in a conditioned state. As stated many times previously, we are kept in a state where our thoughts are under the control of our training and conditioning. Therefore, it is only when our left brain is dampened or suppressed that we catch glimpses of what 'really' is. You may even 'see' something that you have never seen before.

At these moments you may feel that you have an infinite number of possibilities of things to do or achieve.

In emergencies the training of the left brain and instinct (rather than intuition) of the right brain may suddenly work as one. When training and instinct work together at speed "time" may suddenly stand still and it may appear as if you are moving in slow motion.

We could say that our left brain is 'short sighted" because it looks at things closely - too closely and with conditioned logic. Therefore it has a limited view of the world.

The right brain in comparison looks for patterns and relationships. Therefore, consider it as having the ability to take a birds-eye view from a great height. It can see storm clouds over the horizon which cannot be seen from ground level. When 'close' to the ground it is easy to miss the proverbial bigger picture.

Further thoughts on intuition.

You will have read about scientists who have been working on a 'problem' for years when suddenly they have the solution. It seems to appear out of nowhere. Is it because when the left, logical, rational or scientific brain becomes tired, bored or bogged down it suddenly switches off and lets alternative ideas appear out of nowhere?

Another scenario: There is a sudden scientific breakthrough after years and years of work - it all suddenly seems **obvious** and clear - it is when the left brain has relaxed, that the right brain says "here is the answer I had it all the time you just did not give me a chance to speak". It could be said that the right brain does not have to think - it simply picks it out of the 'ether.'

In the 'western' world schools, universities and formal training have, in general and historically, focussed on the left brain. Let us say that the left brain is always in a hurry. It wants more speed, more money, a bigger faster car, 300 TV channels (watch one channel while 3 films playing on other channels are simultaneously being recorded in the background. Do most people actually get round to watching those 3 films?)

Let us also say that the right brain enjoys art, beautiful views, compassion, tolerance and acceptance, and importantly that it 'slows a person down' and in doing so dampens the extravagances and rush to often 'nowhere" of the left brain.

INTRODUCTION II

1. PERCEPTION

The various ideas discussed in this book are aimed at helping you to learn to perceive yourself. That is, help you see how you react to situations and how to view yourself in relation to others and the world at large in as objective* a manner as possible.

{* We could argue that there is no such thing as objectivity. However, for now, we will use it in its traditional way}

Three of the many principles that form part of this process and which are common to many indigenous peoples (untainted by western values) are: humility, respect for one-self and *all* things, and knowing ones place in the scale of creation. For many, it is effort that never stops.

We would all like a mental and emotional awakening which is not only possible but is natural to the environment in which we live and whatever our background. It is not an easy task no matter what the popular novels and videos may depict. However, by daily practice effort can turn into pleasure.

2. CONSCIOUSNESS

What's it all about?

Consciousness & Similar Thoughts

Consciousness is more than seeing auras, feeling energy or transmitting.

Millions of people and entire nations (e.g. Aborigines of Australia) throughout history have believed in an 'exchange of energy' between minds, mind to the body and mind to the world.

In the so called western world the word 'consciousness' has become very popular but at the same time very ambiguous as there are many definitions and interpretations of the word.

One of the non-daily assignments that I suggest is that you undertake research or start a project to look at 'consciousness' or similar words from the perspective of indigenous peoples or groups such as, for example, Hindus or Australian Aboriginals or North American Indians, or Buddhists or Sufis.

In other words question everything you read about or hear about. Do not accept blindly what you read or what you are initially told.

Start a scrap book or open a file and collect all the information that you can gather from the internet (not as reliable as you may think) and books, or join a group or groups who follow a particular philosophy or culture. Once you come across a view(s) or a philosophy that you feel comfortable with, incorporate that philosophy, view or practices in your daily life. Combine various approaches if they work for you. Do not feel you are restricted by one approach.

Do not immediately become 'passionate' or obsessive about a specific view or set of views and do not disregard the views of others or consider them as inferior.

3. Materialism

Financial success is the yardstick by which many gauge success. Some financially successful people (not all) and those related to them tend to attribute special powers to themselves based on their financial strength. They are suddenly smart about *all* aspects of life and if you do not have as much money as they have the attitude may be, 'how on earth can you know what *they* know'.

If you get into a simple discussion with another person and this person adopts the age old tactics of 'attack' and 'put down' because they feel it is necessary to 'win' the discussion – simply smile and SO. Never discuss SO with anyone you are in conversation with. It is not something that is obvious or overt. It is simply something that you do

5. Nutrition

Although nutrition (not included in this book) is critical to your well-being sometimes the problem with alternative/complementary/holistic healthcare is that it places an over emphasis upon herbs, vitamins, potions, on issues such as organic versus non-organic, the newest technology or the latest 'body-worker' technique or training programme (which sometimes can be completed over a weekend).

6. Non-locality

What is at issue is respect for one's participation in a relationship with oneself, others and all matter in the universe – "It is the creation of a reverence or respect for the universe and all that is in the universe that allows the power of healing to develop in one-self."

According to Bertrand Russell, "It would appear that knowledge concerning the universe as a whole is not to be obtained by metaphysics, and that the supposed proofs that, in virtue of the laws of logic, such and such things must exist and such and such others cannot, are not capable of surviving a critical scrutiny"

That is, an 'only' logical or local mind is linear and therefore restrictive. Adopting the attitude 'anything is possible' has led to experiments in nonlocal interactions that show that the past is not fixed but can alter according to present conditions and that the effects of empathic bonding transcend space and time.

Another way to describe non-locality is to say that a person can be instantaneously affected by events that he or she is unaware of and which take place at a distance from that person.

Non-locality is therefore a property of time and space and suggests that all of space-time is available to one's consciousness. However it is a consciousness or level of consciousness that most people are unaware of although it is possible for them to achieve nonlocal minds. It is a matter of tuning into the consciousness of the universe by being open and loving to nature and the universe.

Experiments have shown that some people are not bound by present time. That is, they have the ability to focus attention on distant points (events) in space-time. This ability is termed, "nonlocal awareness".

Laboratory experiments by Alain Aspect support non-locality. He has experimentally shown that entangled particles (pairs of appropriately prepared atomic particles), even though spatially separate, do not operate independently of each other. That is, an object over there does care about what you do to another object over here irrespective of the distance between the two.

It must be noted that entangled particles (used in experiments) are specially laboratory prepared particles that do not acquire their measured properties independently. A single particle that is split in two will result in two particles that both contain identical measurable properties (entangled particles).

What has non-locality to do with health?

Gifted 'healers' over many thousands of years and today can influence the conditions of individuals (subjects) who are physically present with the healers and also subjects who are distant from them.

How does this happen? Popular literature says that it is because the healer's thoughts and intentions are linked to nature and the universe, and that he or she can connect to subjects via nonlocal connections. These connections enable the thoughts and intentions of the 'healer' to influence the condition of the subject. Studies in distant healing and intercessory prayer reveal that the nonlocal mind is intimately connected with compassion, and deep caring. Many hold the view based on various experiments that love and empathy, operating through nonlocal mind, can literally change the world.

Energy transfer: The Kaznacheyev Experiments

Vlail Kaznacheyev (Institute for Clinical and Experimental Medicine in Novosibirsk, Russia.)

Kaznacheyev undertook experiments with twin cell cultures that lead to an understanding of disease and healing that is not understood or used by traditional medicine. The experiments show that (any) cellular disease, virus or cellular death can be transmitted electromagnetically and transferred into another healthy cell.

In the experiments, two sealed containers were placed side by side, with a thin optical window separating them. The two containers were completely environmentally shielded except for the optical coupling.

A tissue was separated into two identical samples, and one sample placed in each of the two halves of the apparatus. The cells in one sample (on one side of the glass) were then subjected to a virus, bacterial infection or chemical poison. This led to disease and death of the exposed cell culture sample.

If the thin optical window was made of ordinary window glass, the uninfected cells on the other side of the window were undamaged and remained healthy. This of course was as expected from an orthodox medical perspective. However, if the thin optical window was made of quartz, something else happened. About 12 hours after the disease appeared in the infected sample, the same features of disease appeared in the uninfected sample.

This startling "infection by optical coupling" occurred in 70-80% of the tests. From an orthodox medical view, these results were unexpected and unheard of.

The Relationship between Life and Non-locality

Since the advent of quantum physics western scientists have gained a deeper understanding of man and his relationship to the universe. However, it has also posed a dilemma for many scientists in that it has brought into question a number of existing beliefs.

For example, past experience and perceptions have proved not always to be valid. Also, the need to question or redefine certain words and concepts has arisen, and (most important) the role of the soul in scientific research has arisen. However, to eastern minds now and in the past these issues are not new. From many eastern perspectives the soul or absolute consciousness is at one with the universe. Therefore, the integration of the spiritual aspects of life with scientific research is not new and should not be a cause of any concern.

This section is a brief introduction to the interrelationships between human consciousness and the universe, and how attitude (as a starting point) can, in some small practical way, lead a person to a better understanding of his or her innermost self.

Millions of people search daily for enlightenment, consciousness (call it whatever you prefer) However, as we all know, enlightenment, consciousness similar to religion is a very personal matter.

In the 2000's it is big business. Many people need a quick fix. It is the age of instant gratification and if you don't know where you are going any video, seminar, the latest book, so called guru will do. How many times have you heard someone say, 'I've read the book, I've seen the film, attended this or that seminar but nothing happened.' Hard to believe, but true. Many people expect instantaneous results after reading a book or watching a video. A seminar or book may provide certain theories or philosophies but may not supply the day to day guidance to help one along the road.

The aim is for you to experience a combination of non-locality and what is commonly nowadays called self-awareness. Nothing new! Both are thousands of years old.

"Consciousness may initially be fleetingly experienced when you develop the ability to hold multiple perceptions of what is happening around you locally and globally, and observe those perceptions from a neutral position as closely as possible." That is, one needs the ability to also observe, in parallel, one's own traditional and conditioned biases.

As and when this happens, non-locality (loosely defined) becomes something that you begin to "think about", consider every day and experience at a gross level."

This view may not be acceptable to readers who are academics and scientists. It is what may be termed 'applied philosophy'. It is an attempt to apply and live the ideas, philosophies that exist or appear out of the 'ether'.

Aldous Huxley views consciousness as the fundamental building blocks of the universe. That is, human beings can access all of the universe through their own consciousness and their 'nonlocal' minds (see the section on non-locality). Certain schools of thought propose that the purpose of life is to 'become one with the universe*'. That is, the purpose of life is to become one with your God, and then help others do the same.

[Consider this term an English translation and possibly a little misleading when used literally]

Hinduism teaches that individual consciousness (Atman) and universal consciousness (Brahman) are one. Physicist, David Bohm says that in the universe there is a collective consciousness (a greater collective mind) with no boundaries of space and time. The Vedas , the oldest spiritual books of India, teach that our bodies appear to be separate from one another but our consciousness is not.

Guide- Daily: Self Observation

"Know thyself"

What does it mean?

To know yourself you must first study yourself.

Self-study requires Self Observation which leads to self-knowledge

As we proceed through the following exercise do not try any form of analysis. Also, even as you observe yourself for days, months even years, do not try any type of formal analysis of what takes place or attempt to draw any conclusions. Simply observe yourself as if you were a third person or an independent observer whose only function is to record what happens without involvement or comment, and without passing judgement.

Assignment guide:

When you adopt new approaches such as SO it is critical that you do not try to analyse what happens when you start to SO. Only observe yourself for days if not months. Do not try to analyse what takes place or attempt to draw any conclusions. Simply observe yourself as if you were a third person or an independent observer who only records what happens without involvement or comment or without passing judgement.

Insight

Alexis Carrol wrote that in order for man to have mental and physiological balance he must enforce a code of conduct upon himself. This conduct was of a moral nature. He also went on to say that very few people (obviously at his time) conducted themselves according to moral ideals.

Interestingly enough the Qur'an says that a person with a clear mind, a healthy body, a clear heart and a clear intellect is able to progress to a higher level and achieve basira (keen insight). From basira emerges marifa which may be described as 'realisation', 'the ultimate knowledge upon which all knowledge rests'.

*Man's possibilities are very great. You cannot conceive
even a shadow of what man is capable of attaining.
But nothing can be attained in sleep.*

*In the consciousness of a sleeping man his illusions,
his 'dreams' are mixed with reality.*

*He lives in a subjective world and he can never escape from it.
And this is why he can never make use of all the powers
he possesses and why he always lives in only a small part of himself.*

G. I. Gurdjieff

*It "is as important for children to release their parents as for the
parents to release their children and for both to try and free the others
from inner debts, judgements and grudges."*

Dr. M. Nicoll

*"[People search for God by the experimental process, but after much
searching they fail. Then they say, 'oh, there is no God. I am God.'
But the Īśopanisad says that one should try to learn about God not
by the experimental process but by hearing. From whom should one
hear? From a shopkeeper? From fanatics? No. One should hear from
those who are dhira. Dhïra means "one whose senses are not agitated
by material influence."]"*

A.C. Bhaktivedanta Swami Prabhupāda

The "Quiet Mind"

Our physical and mental health depends on the degree to which we control our thoughts. Our minds are constantly filled with words, images and sounds from the 'outside', which control and influence what we think, how we think and how we perceive the world and ourselves.

In order to discover who we really are we must eliminate fear, coveting, craving and judgement, and develop a 'quiet mind' that blocks all the advertising that is designed to create needs that eventually make us 'suffer'. Again, certain schools propose that desires, judgemental attitudes and attachments to material objects are the cause of the world's sufferings.

The truly quiet mind is aware of 'Self' and can experience an overwhelming peace and connection with man and the universe. When the mind is quiet and open it has the opportunity to be overwhelmed by love. It is what is termed "undifferentiated awareness' Unbounded and undifferentiated awareness (sunyata) is the teaching of emptiness (no fear, no cravings, no jealousy, no judgement, no wants, no ego).

Perspectives on life

Please consider the following questions in relation to your own perspectives and beliefs.

Are time and space (as words or concepts) elements of man's own creation and do they have no real meaning except in our minds, based on what we have been conditioned to think?

Is the inner self or consciousness part of the infinite and therefore not restricted to our physical body?

What is love?

Once you have formulated your thoughts with respect to the above consider the following:

> Consciousness is the fundamental building block of the universe; human beings can access the entire universe through their own consciousness and nonlocal (see below) mind, and the purpose of life is to become one with the universe – *Aldous Huxley*
>
> Individual consciousness (Atman) and universal consciousness (Brahman) are one – *Hinduism*
>
> Human beings are joined to each other and all creation – *Rabbi Lawrence Kushner*
>
> Space and time are but modes of human perception, not attributes of the physical world – *Immanuel Kant.*
>
> Ananda: We have within us everything we could look for – *Hinduism*
>
> Love in the Buddhist sense is not about romance or bodies; it is about wisdom wedded to compassion.
>
> "This is the secret of creation. What you think you create"

Attitude as a Creative Tool

Attitude and its development as a creative tool are crucial to learning how to use the powers of the mind. The creativity of the mind can be engaged and developed by choosing an attitude and cultivating that attitude. Therefore, an attitude is creative and creativity is an attitude.

The ideas in our minds, our perspectives of the world and people, and our expectations create our experiences and become self-fulfilling

Deciding upon an Attitude

Is the glass half empty?

Is the glass half full?

Or

Is it half empty and half full?

Or

Who cares!

Depending on how you want to look at the glass decides an attitude - your attitude. Remember you have a choice on deciding which one you select. If your attitude is 'positive' and you decide the glass is half full your attitude will lead your mind and it's perceptions in one direction. If you decide the glass is half empty your mind and it's perceptions will go in another direction.

Therefore, your ideas are a function of your attitude. An attitude is how you approach a problem or situation. An attitude can also be an expression on your face. Your posture and your expression often express your attitude towards the world. Your attitude is your orientation. It is your way of interacting with people, situations and with life itself.

If we say that a person's reality is based upon how his attitudes influence and direct the patterns of his thoughts we could say that attitude is creative. But more importantly it influences which ideas will govern what you notice and how you understand or perceive what you notice.

How you approach a situation or problem influences how the situation or problem responds to your approach. Your attitude is a key factor in the creation of your reality.

Exercise 2. ATTITUDE

Attitude has four 'Critical Success Factors' or variables that play a key role in supporting the development of Attitude

RESPECT

Treat others as you would like them to treat you. The very moment you treat others (one way or another) you are setting up the way you will be treated later.

PATIENCE

Patience, particularly with others, develops insights and a deeper understanding of a situation or problem, as well as a deeper understanding of yourself.

DECISIONS

Make decisions by listening within. Make decisions based on what your inner self tells you (intuition), not your personality or rational mind.

IDEALS

An 'ideal' life can only be created once an ideal pattern has been established. Only once ideals have been established is it possible to focus on thought patterns, which are consistent with those ideals.

Do you have choices to make, or 'if you are lost (in life) where do you want to go?' Begin by knowing your ideals. An ideal is a standard by which we measure the value of something, and which may develop or change over time. When you question what you want out of life or make choices, you are testing your ideals.

Ideals carefully and practically chosen generate ideas and the combination of the two creates reality.

Developing a Self Reliant Attitude

In all problem situations it is important to cast off or reject any feelings of helplessness. An attitude or feelings of victimisation by circumstances must be altered to an attitude of self-reliance.

An attitude of self-reliance is one that rejects being the passive pawn of outside forces and one which chooses how it will respond to circumstances. For example, if a person is hopelessly in debt he or she can adopt an attitude of victimization (it's not my fault). An attitude of victimization focuses on the pressures of circumstances and is one that has a depressing and numbing effect on a person. A self-reliant attitude, however, focuses on the available choices: for example, how shall I manage the money I have available?

No matter what the situation you always have the choice of attitude of how you respond to the situation. A judgemental attitude confines a person to a perceived helpless situation. By eliminating all judgement you are able to accept what is happening without being overwhelmed by the situation. Accepting a situation does not mean that you 'give in' to the situation. It only means that you recognize and understand the situation and appreciate all the implications related to the situation or problem.

If you hold the attitude, "I can make a difference" it is possible to take a role in determining or influencing the outcome of a situation rather than being a passive participant. People, who believe that they can exert some control over a situation or influence the process will persist in influencing the situation, and will not stop when confronted by obstacles, and are less stressed by negative events.

If a person has no sense of personal control then he or she is hostage to circumstances. However, a person who can or may learn to control the situation, even in only a small way, can eventually take full or partial control of the situation or environment.

An exercise in creativity – Think laterally.

Start at one dot and travel to all the dots using only four straight lines. Do not lift the pencil once you have started.

```
•   •   •

•   •   •

•   •   •
```

Miscellaneous

In general it is often stated in literature particularly in sport that it is important to believe in "Self" and to adopt an attitude "Anything is Possible." However, these two attitudes require both practice and a balanced or realistic approach.

During periods of relaxation that include specific breathing exercises, it is possible to bring the sympathetic and para-sympathetic nervous systems into 'balance' if, (for example) a person was 'sympathetic dominant' before the exercise. This exercise has a beneficial effect on the immune system, endocrine and limbic systems. {Note: This is only a very brief and basic description}

Relaxation exercises combined with breathing exercises can have a beneficial effect on heart rate variability (HRV). Also, when combined with a mantra it may bring about other subtle changes which will vary from person to person.

For certain people the incorporation of relaxation techniques combined with SO & SR in daily life will help develop new visions or perspectives not only of themselves but also of their environment. Also, the process must be effortless, a person must want to do so – he or she cannot be forced. It could be said that the practice of SO needs to be driven by a strong desire to take control of one's thoughts and actions. SO driven by a strong yet covert desire will slowly and automatically (in the background) eliminate the manifestation of negative thought, and negative actions and reactions particularly to sudden, unexpected events.

The daily elimination of expression of 'unpleasant emotions' ranging from not liking the weather to passing 'negative' comments about people, organizations or situations is one of the ways in which a man can change 'himself or his habits without creating other undesirable habits.'

The greatest thing in all education is to make the nervous system our ally instead of our enemy.

– WILLIAM JAMES

Illness or Dis-ease

A few daily activities that affect our health:

Lifestyle
(Consider your lifestyle in relation to your health)

What and *when* we eat

What and *when* we drink

Posture, movement, breathing

Environment - House, workplace,..

Associations – Relationships with people, groups

Attitude - Negative emotions, negative thinking

Criticism – identification

Imagination

'Finite' views

What and when we think

What and when we speak

Self-justification

There is an over emphasis on nutritional fads and new so called systems of wellness or health. 'New' systems appear almost monthly and are all aimed at profiting from the high level of 'confusion' that exists globally.

Confusion creates fear. Fear creates, for example, 'stress', anxiety and jealousy. Chronic stress may result in high levels of cortisol which make us susceptible to conditions ranging from arthritis to depression. It also makes us susceptible to infectious diseases.

BODY CHEMISTRY

According to ME Page (1894-1983) a dentist and researcher in 'balancing body chemistry' toxicity in the body is the main reason for disease. His view was that 'modern' lifestyles result in toxicity in the body.

His view was that a person could have a 'perfect meal' that included all the balanced nutrients required. However, if the meal was eaten in conjunction with a carbonated soft drink the sugar in the soft drink could cause problems. The sugar could block the body from getting the nutrients supplied by the food or could make the nutrients toxic to the body. When this happens the body is susceptible to external stressors. (sugar comes in many forms and guises)

His research is 'in-line' with the research of people such as Bernard (1813-1879), Bechamp (1816-1908), Enderlein (1872-1968), Rife, Reich Cannon and Naessens.

Health Critical Success Factors: The role of enzymes and biological imbalances are obviously important and are covered in the workshop together with the difference between slow and fast healers.

BIO-FEEDBACK

The endocrine system (in particular the Hypothalamus) helps maintain balance within the body (homeostasis). It also controls or influences such things as sleeping, eating, drinking, physical and sexual activity, and the neuro-chemical regulation of such diverse behaviours as heart rate, respiration and glandular activity.

The direction, depth and nature of our thoughts have a direct impact on our physical body. Thoughts and emotions influence the HPA (Hypothalamus, Pituitary, Adrenals) axis which in turn influences our immune system in either a positive or negative way depending on the nature of the thoughts or emotions. Let us say that pleasant thoughts produce harmonizing energy or information that not only allows the various organs of our body to operate in a most effective and efficient way, but also allows for clear and unambiguous communication between the organs. Disruptive or angry emotional thoughts will have the opposite effect.

In a parallel fashion and from an energetic perspective certain types of energy or information can disrupt the normal flow and polarity of the electromagnetic flows in and around the body. Disruption or modification of these flows can result in dis-ease or organ malfunction. Intense, negative emotions such as anger, fear or jealousy, if suppressed for long periods, can result in dis-ease or contribute to ill-health.

Forgiveness and Fear

There may be many reasons for, or causes of, conflicting, negative thoughts or emotions that may disrupt or disturb a person's life. Sudden emotional shocks can result in illness and even life threatening disease. An approach of tolerance and acceptance ['not easy', you may say], if it becomes part and parcel of your approach to life, is often the key to resolving interpersonal conflict. Not only will it prevent conflict but it will also create and maintain harmonizing thoughts to dampen and then eliminate the disruptive energy that results from an old conflict or event.

Without forgiveness (of oneself or of someone else) the process is flawed and will fail. Why, because it is a critical factor in human physiological and mental harmony.

The combination of nutrition, integrative therapies, relaxation and the development of awareness all lead a person to wholeness of body and spirit that can prevent or heal both physical and emotional conditions.

Forgiveness and the elimination of fear are important factors but sometimes ignored by both the patient and the doctor in the "treatment of the whole person."

The emphasis of this book is on self-awareness and the workshop is on all the factors involved in the treatment of the whole person

"Life is Short and the Art is Long;
Occasion Fleeting;
Intervention Perilous;
Judgment Difficult."

Hippocrates

Jay Carson is a graduate of Glasgow College of Technology, Scotland and Palmer College of Chiropractic, Davenport, USA.

www.ingramcontent.com/pod-product-compliance
Lightning Source LLC
Chambersburg PA
CBHW071311040426
42444CB00009B/1980